# Dad, What's Wrong with Sophie?

## By Lulu

 Illustrations by Karyna Unsovich

"Dedicated to every animal that creeps, caws, gallops, crawls, barks, and meows- we don't deserve you."

Diego's eyes sprang open. *Today* was the day; it was his birthday, and he was turning seven years old. He lay in his warm bed, imagining the exciting gift he might receive.

Would it be a new gaming system? Or, maybe it was that awesome remote-controlled airplane he'd been telling his mom about every day for months?

Diego's excitement bubbled in his belly as he jumped out of bed and skipped down the stairs. In the kitchen, Diego's mom and dad greeted him with joyous shouts of "Happy birthday!" followed by big bear hugs.

"I made your favorite breakfast," his mom said, pouring syrup over pancakes and placing them in front of him. The pancakes were covered with chocolate chips, forming a melting smiley face. Diego giggled and wolfed them down.

"Tonight, we'll celebrate your special day," his mom cheerfully reminded him as she cleaned the kitchen. "That's when we'll give you your birthday gift." Diego felt the excitement bubble up again. "Can I open it now?" he pleaded.

"No, you need to wait until tonight," his mom gently reminded him. Diego sighed, dragging his feet as he climbed the stairs to get dressed for school. How could he possibly wait until tonight?

At school, Diego kept thinking about the gift he would receive that night and how the day couldn't go by any slower! The only thing that helped him get through the long day was everyone wishing him a happy birthday (and the double-chocolate cupcakes his mom had sent to school).

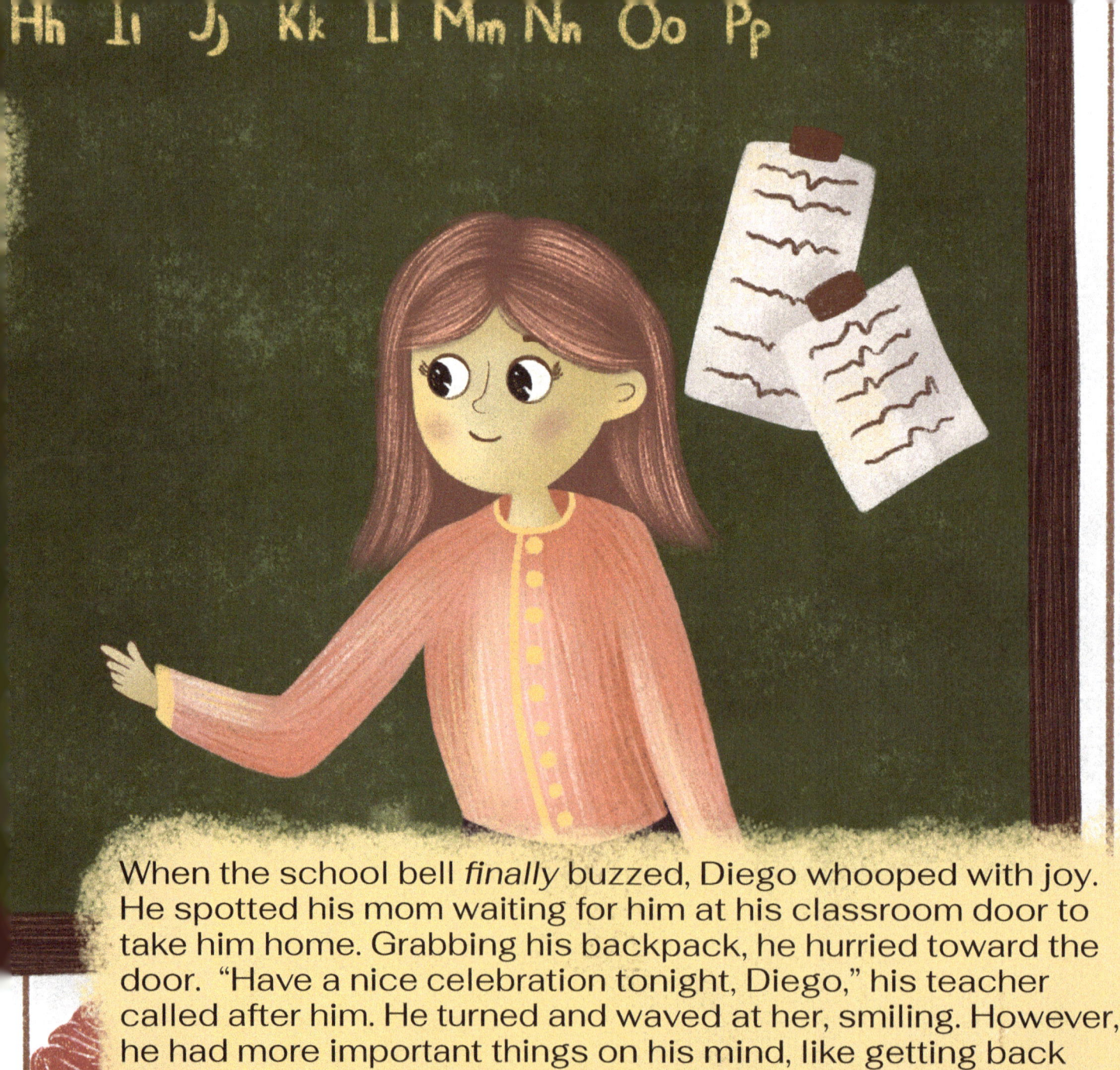

When the school bell *finally* buzzed, Diego whooped with joy. He spotted his mom waiting for him at his classroom door to take him home. Grabbing his backpack, he hurried toward the door. "Have a nice celebration tonight, Diego," his teacher called after him. He turned and waved at her, smiling. However, he had more important things on his mind, like getting back home to start his birthday celebration and opening his gift. He felt like he might burst from all the day's excitement!

At home, Diego sat at the dinner table, admiring the birthday decorations his mom had carefully hung around the dining room. He tapped the balloons in the middle of the table with his fingers and giggled as they bounced around.

Soon, his mom set down his favorite dinner, pepperoni pizza. He was on his second piece when his dad got up and said, "I'll be right back." He left the table and headed into the living room.

When his dad returned, Diego saw he was carrying a large cardboard box, which he very carefully set on the floor. He jumped out of his chair and ran to where his dad had stopped with the box. "Is that my birthday gift?" he asked, excitedly dancing around the room.

Laughing, his mom and dad both exclaimed, "YES!" Diego couldn't imagine what might be in the large box. He slowly lifted the long top flaps that were lying loosely, untaped. "What could this be?" he thought, slowly leaning over the box to peek inside.

As his eyes took in the furry contents of the box, they widened until they couldn't open any farther. A puppy was peering up at him from inside, with soft brown eyes and fluffy golden fur! "A PUPPY!" Diego shrieked, his eyes brimming with tears. "This is the best birthday gift ever!" he declared.

"What are you going to name her?" his dad asked.
Without missing a beat, Diego answered, "I'm going to call her Sophie." He scooped her out of the box and snuggled her tightly against his chest while she licked his face with sloppy dog kisses. Everyone laughed with joy.

Diego danced around the house with Sophie. Soon, she was chasing him, and her barking and his giggles filled the house. Diego spent most of his free time training Sophie and teaching her good dog manners and new tricks. Everyone was surprised at how quickly she learned each one.

"I have the smartest dog in the world," Diego said, hugging her neck. With her excited barks, Sophie seemed to agree. "The dog treats probably helped a little, too," Diego's dad said as he chuckled.

Diego's and Sophie's bond grew stronger as they aged together. Some of his friends tried to tell him Sophie was just a dog, but Diego insisted she was a member of his family. When he was happy, her tail would wag in joy with him.

When he was sad, she would nestle her fuzzy head in his lap, filling him with comfort and peace. Sophie was more than a pet; she was his best friend who loved him unconditionally, and nothing could ever change his mind.

For Diego and Sophie, family holiday celebrations were some of the year's best highlights, with Halloween being their favorite.

As they walked through the neighborhood collecting treats, the neighbors "oohed" and "ahhed" over how awesome they looked together.

Their next favorite holiday was Thanksgiving. The house was always filled with the delicious aromas of turkey and side dishes, and the scents held the promise of a full belly. Sophie sat patiently next to Diego, her big brown eyes fixed on all the delicious food, covering the dinner table.

Her tail thumped impatiently against the floor as Diego snuck her bits of his favorite foods– until his mom or dad caught him. Then, they all laughed while Sophie tried to win them over with playful barks, hoping for more table scraps.

Christmas was always a joyous time for Diego and Sophie, with the house and tree glowing with multi-colored lights and glittering homemade ornaments.

They snuggled by the crackling fireplace, its warmth wrapping around them like a soft blanket as Diego made a Christmas list of the latest toys and technolgy he thought he needed. Gradually, the cozy heat would make both of them sleepy.

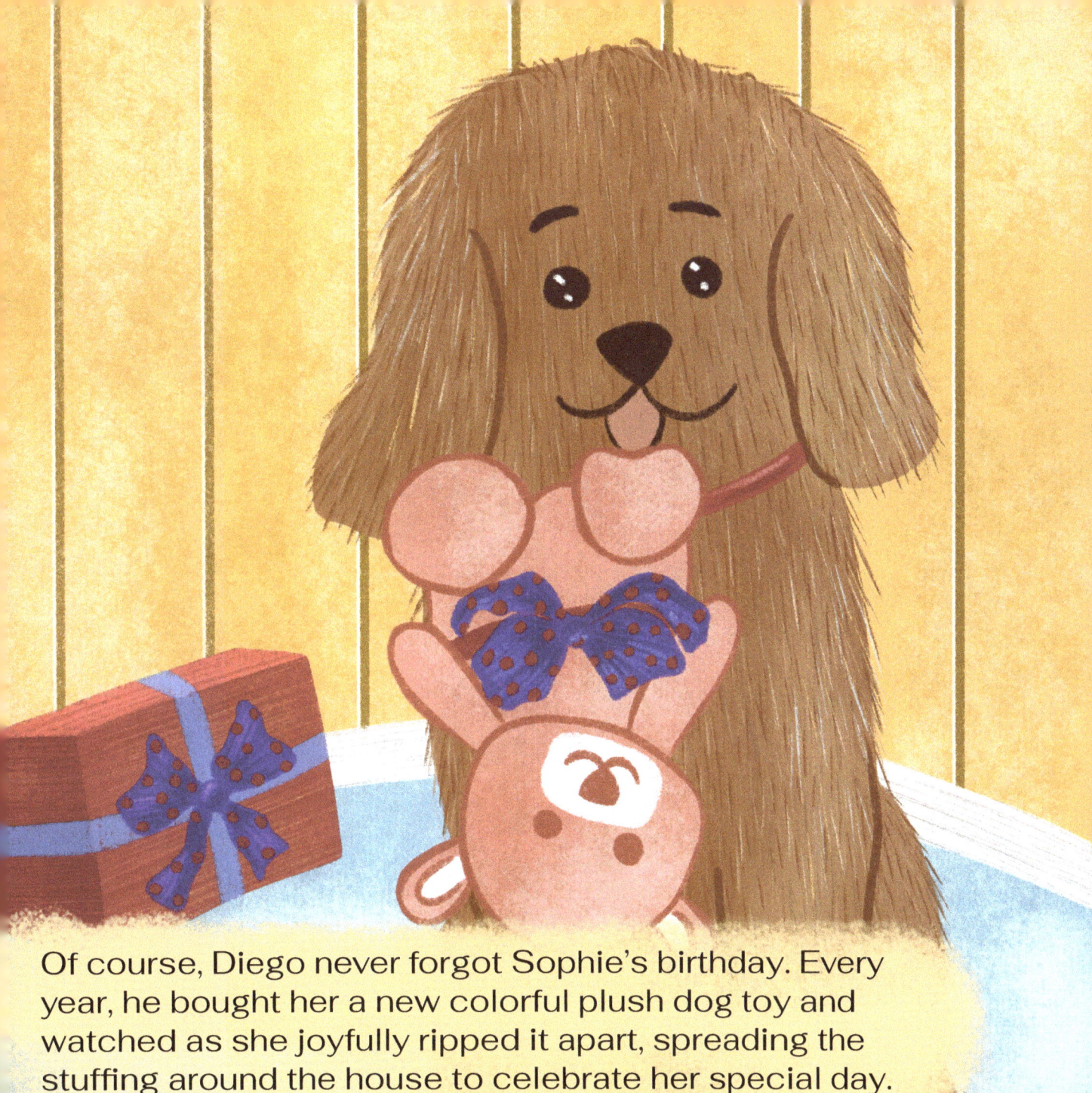

Of course, Diego never forgot Sophie's birthday. Every year, he bought her a new colorful plush dog toy and watched as she joyfully ripped it apart, spreading the stuffing around the house to celebrate her special day.

Before bedtime, Sophie gobbled down the delicious yogurt cookie that Diego and his mom made just for her. Diego always thought he could see a smile on her face as she fell asleep on her special day.

Sadly, as the years passed, Sophie began to show signs of aging. Touches of white began to peek out of her once-vibrant gold fur, and her eyes grew cloudy. Diego noticed her steps becoming stiffer and slower, so he started carrying her up the stairs when she struggled.

When she no longer wanted to play fetch, he sat quietly by her side, running his hand over her soft fur, assuring her that his love for her was as strong as the first day he had scooped her out of that cardboard box.

One day, Diego noticed something very different about Sophie after coming home from school. She seemed more sluggish, and her eyes were half closed, almost like she was in pain. Worried, he went and found his dad.

With a tremble in his voice, Diego asked,
"Dad, what's wrong with Sophie?"

Gently, Diego's dad sat him down and explained that Sophie was getting old, and sometimes when our beloved pets grow old, they become weak or sick.

Diego felt a big lump in his throat, and his eyes filled with tears as he realized Sophie might not be with him much longer. He wrapped his arms tightly around her neck and buried his face in her fur.

Diego and his dad took Sophie to the vet for a wellness check, where the vet advised them to keep her as comfortable as possible over the next several weeks. They created a cozy spot for her in the living room with her favorite blanket and toys, so she could be near the family. Diego even made a bed in the living room so that he could stay close to her. During those quiet nights, he gently reminded her of their many adventures, softly petting her until they both fell asleep.

Despite the family's thoughtful and loving efforts, Sophie's health continued to decline over the next few weeks.

Finally, one day Diego's dad approached him, and through many tears, shared the sad truth: it was time to say goodbye to Sophie.

The difficult day came. With great sadness, Diego and his parents headed to the veterinarian's office.

Diego held Sophie close, taking in her smell. Tears slid down his face as he whispered soft, loving words to his best friend.

Surrounded by their love, in the stillness of the quiet room at the veterinarian's office, Sophie peacefully closed her eyes for the last time. Diego's dad stood beside him, gently laying a hand on his shoulder for support.

Although Diego could feel the warmth of his dad's hand, he still felt cold and numb. He'd never felt pain like this before, an overwhelming sense of loss that made his heart heavy.

The days following Diego's sad goodbye to Sophie were very difficult for Diego and his family. They shared many stories, some of which made them laugh and some of which made them cry, but all of the memories made them grateful for the joyous time and love that Sophie had brought into their lives over the years.

Diego and his parents decided to create a memorial, a special place in their backyard where Diego could go and reflect on the memories and the sweet bond he'd shared with his dog. They planted a small evergreen tree in Sophie's memory, a token to remind them of the loyalty that she had shown them throughout the years.

Every time her face appeared in his thoughts, Diego sat by Sophie's tree. As the evergreen tree grew, the deep ache in Diego's heart lessened and was replaced with gratitude. He would never forget his furry companion and knew her spirit would live forever in his heart.

"Thank you, Sophie, for three beautiful years."

www.ingramcontent.com/pod-product-compliance
Lightning Source LLC
Chambersburg PA
CBHW041154120626
46547CB00020B/3216